OTHERLIGHT

YESYES BOOKS

Portland, OR

This is an Early Edition available only through YesYes Books,
the author, and select sellers.

Cover & Interior Design: Alban Fischer
Project lead: KMA Sullivan

ISBN 978-1-936919-95-6
Printed in the United States of America

Published by YesYes Books
1631 NE Broadway St #121
Portland, OR 97232
yesyesbooks.com

KMA Sullivan, Publisher
Joanna Acevedo, Assistant Editor
Brandon Courtney, Senior Editor, Operations
Alban Fischer, Graphic Designer
A. Tony Jerome, Assistant Editor
Karah Kemmerly, Assistant Editor
Jill Kolongowski, Manuscript Copy Editor
James Sullivan, Assistant Editor, Audio Books
Gale Marie Thompson, Senior Editor, Book Development

CONTENTS

"You are like God. We pray to Him, and He answers No.
Then we pray to Him to rescind the *no*, and he doesn't answer at all."

—EMILY DICKINSON

"What we cannot accomplish, what
 is denied to love
     what we have lost in the anticipation—
                         a descent follows,
 endless and indestructible."

—WILLIAM CARLOS WILLIAMS

THE LAKE WILL WAIT

I know it scares you when I say *I'm not afraid to die.*

      Still, you go on listening,
as birds plummet into the grass—fortune
teller, pharmacist, archangel, canary—

who taught me suffering—
how to talk to the sky,
                how to ask it *what's the worst thing that could happen?*

I try to guess
      when birds will stop making meteors of their bodies—

when will you stop believing me when I say *I'm getting better*
about taking my meds,
        when I say *I stopped thinking of jumping a long time ago?*

I disappoint you. When I talk about the comforting gloom
        of a birdless sky, that lake
of quiet, I hear my own shadow

call it want. Call it impossible—
        to heal, to understand,

to shake a ghost bird back to life in its cage, impossible to build
cages under every bridge I'll ever cross—you can't

        make someone want to be alive no matter how hard you shake them.

BOUND FOR

Lightning so angry half the lights floated
blacked, flickered, came back

      and I filled my bathtub with water *in case of a true outage,*
an emergency-emergency. Why were you

at the bottom of those pools that—in the dark—
beware me of blood? I look to the water. I see

you clawing at your own throat,

strangers promising
            He's in a better place.

      What better—what life
after this—too late

for naloxone, too late for Heaven,

new earth. I sit here perpetually
         inventing lives more terrifying to live—

as if reality were not enough. I hope you never know

how far, how deep
my grief dragged me—the everydayness

of walking empty

                grocery stores, parking lots, quiet fluorescents,
the quiet telephone.

I think that I am alive—once,

                    you said *Lobsters,*
you said *something with their chromosomes,*
you said *the only thing time does for them is grow—*

I think that I am alive now
because you are not.

If there is a world in which the dead speak, let them
tell me what it's worth—your name
so difficult to say.

DROWNING DOES NOT LOOK LIKE DROWNING

Tonight, I wade the deep end.

Wrapped in your white bedsheet, I blur,
I forget my meds,

you love the way that sets me free—
my repeated: *Hurry.*

> *Be older. Be honest with me.*

How long do you plan on living?
Look up at me.
Tell me how we can live

  our deepest lives underwater.

If I were a child I would invent some game.
I would say the water rising
over our heads is part of it—

I would cover my mouth like chloroform.
    I would close my eyes,

I would shout your name until my hands found
your body.

If this was a game I would pretend
to be wearing a dress, I would pin a note to it:

Do with me what you will.

Tonight, I am listening
    for your voice in the water.
I'm looking back
    for our ghosts, the ghosts of children

pulling us through our pasts
like quiet,
like a photograph of a window that gives up only
    the everyday blue of sky.

I feel that lack, I feel a body pass just beyond my outstretched palm.
Our childhood game, finished,

        changed from *how long can you stay*
        underwater to
                    can you hold your breath until you black out?

Underwater, I hear the telephone.
Is it you?

And if it is you
what do you want?
What more
        can I give you?
When you call me
where

        do you call me from?

If I answer could I answer,
could I

even begin

    to answer:

      Where are all the fish—

          we the stylishly drowned?

PSYCHOTHERAPY: PROLOGUE

"What brings you here today?"

As if I could explain that easily

when there are places on this earth that grow so wild
even our maker was not sure where to begin.

And how could I hope
to begin knowing

what it will cost me to say what I really mean?
When you see me in so much pain I am unable to speak

will you call me ice?
Will you rip my life wide open?

It's a lie—

how everyone says a story can only begin
one of two ways:

with someone coming to town,

with someone leaving.

"In your own words, what is the problem you are seeking help for?"

How will I recognize a problem? *What is a problem?*

How the moon shakes the dice of the water?
How I wake to a phone in my hand?

Am I dialing?

Is it ringing?

How true it is that I am afraid of answering

or who
answers. The possibility of what
could be said is

cheap vodka thrown over a fire.

What is lost can never be gotten back.
How solemn, how terrible, how terrifying—

but I am looking forward to the way a city falls in love as it burns,
to the day when I can't remember him at all.

No matter if the voice on the phone says

"Come with me. I need to ask you a few questions—"

"Have you ever been diagnosed with a mental illness prior to this date?"

Illness is just the story we tell ourselves
to justify
the horror of not in pain or on pain—
    the pain between sleep and no sleep.

Illness only means something if you allow it
to repeat to you
what an old boyfriend said to me:

You are. You are a crazy bitch, aren't you?

"Describe for me your relationships with others."

When we fucked at his parents' house he held his hand over my mouth.

"How many days out of the last month have you felt depressed?"

500   milligrams of Wellbutrin

            helps half the time,
                stops working—

I can't decide

which I prefer: the depression or the frenzy
of sleepless birds on film. Like it matters

how often in this life do we get the things we ask for?

Serves me right for thinking
there are perfect lives and that I could begin one
without consequence, without loss.

Depression never looks like what you are looking for.
I am trying to change

what scares me into something a stranger
might find beautiful.

I put on a dress. I go out. I laugh. I live—
I pretend like I'm living. I say
stranger, make me real
to myself, take me home,
look at what a nice girl I am.

Let me call depression *desire* then—
I sell that better version of myself
that is not aching apart. I am
holding it together. I am making it okay.

I am making you want what I have.

"If you could look into a crystal ball, if you could tell the future—what would you see?"

a man holds his hand over my mouth

"How are you sleeping these days?"

What sleep?
All night, I turn

though the city is quiet like snow

falling through a mineshaft
After hours of vodka,

sleep's pull is irresistible,

the force of star's collapse toward gravity,

but still my body asks *do I know you?*

Doesn't matter if I drug myself

who else is the anxious spirit of this world that must go over
and over
what it already knows

what waits on the other side of the door of sleep? I know well
that this isn't going well,
that everyone else also has

before dawn—no stars—
I will try again
              and if I do

ever sleep again,
please don't wake me.

I want to see where I go.

DYNAMITE

A ghost leaves your body and never returns—
this is a lie.

      A person has to earn
the right to forget.

What if, from now on,
I subscribe to that specific turn-of-the-century-belief
         that illness is caused by spirits—

use this to explain why
      I tried to protect your body with mine: *My life for yours,*
remember?
No matter where that promise would have taken me
         I would've made it. I would've

  slept forever for you to live.
I'm sorry I lived

      through what you could not.
Do you remember the earth before this earth,

your birthplace on fire?
      Now my body is kindling owned by your ghost. If I become anything
let there be no stopping it

      let there be grace in living thigh to thigh with ghosts.

That's the thing about using ghosts as explanations for illness:
you hold them close enough and they become a part of you,

    long enough and you forget they are there, they become an apology,
they rip the roof off of the sky.

THE NAME OF YOUR HAND IS ICE

When you are first introduced to your depression,

your depression tries to rip your teeth from the bone,
it snaps doves' necks
      outside your bedroom window.

You call it sky and it calls you

  crazy fucking bitch, why are you here?

     When you feel out of control,
you think of a boyfriend who once slapped you

     cold
you were a dream
     violence could solve—

you blame him
     for knocking the cycle of sad, manic, sad into you.
You asked him
    what did you do that for?

The city answers by trying to suffocate you.
     It boils your brain against your skull.
The heat drags you deeper.
You reason

     it will get worse. Tonight,

you stand in front of a dark mirror and slap yourself across the face
        until your face is an open lake
filling with blood.

You mean to promise, you mean to wake,
you mean to open
        your mouth for the sky's hands.

There are reasons for everything, you tell the sky—

how badly you miss the sun.

TELEPHONE

I am beginning to view the body as a well I could shout *Hello*   *Hello* into
call it a mistake   hang up out of alarm   because *tell me* what you thought
you were doing answering when you've been dead five whole years? And is
it really you?   How have you kept alive?   What have you grown down
there in the gloom of after like salt?   Perhaps I should say mine   the body
is a salt mine   And I never call but you answer anyway   Was it ever
cheerful?   The sound called ringing   Don't talk to me   *please*
don't tell me I need you disoriented   buried alive   clawing your way
up from the mouth of a cave to show me the way home and *tell me*   what
does this even mean?

Tell me to spread open my palms   cut another deck of cards face up   these
lines arch me far from home   I cannot stop from coming   my fate   are
you what brings me here   my annihilating angel?   Everyone knows that
when you die   you learn everything   so tell me about my life   Tell me
about my sun line   my one day call me bitch   I love that hands-on
unmaking and making I must impossibly bloom forth   that tallest mountain
I dial the dead and you answer   Hand me the telephone   give me your ice
your hour of starving   your naked   *promise me*   I will die dark haired
and one day you and I will burn buildings together for warmth   *Speak to*
me   Tell me about me   I want to be believed

NEW SHOES ON A DEAD HORSE

Imagine him half-drunk at the treeline
in someone's sister's boyfriend's yard.
In the city after dark,
              never truly dark.
Imagine his Goodwill sweater, his face as he turns to face
the trees.
Imagine there are trees at all

to beg him darkward—*don't turn back.*
Forget

your given life.
I said I loved you.

       What did you hear?

OTHERLIGHT

A need in me makes me descend
that long drop to water,

the abyss at the end of a line—
            I don't know if I mean cocaine or poem.

        It is so quiet.

PSYCHOPHARMACOLOGY: HALF LIFE

"What brings you here today?"

      The official cause of death was overdose.
                One of his brothers called to tell me.
      I couldn't understand over the sobbing

      all I caught was "blood, salt, angels, brain floating,
                do something to save us—"

      I'll never get the full story.
      I'll never be
          certain but I've seen enough blood
      roll back through glass vials,
      enough blood rising—no stopping it—

      heard enough love stories end
          through walls of cheap apartments to be sure

      it wasn't as simple
        as falling asleep and never waking up.

"What is important to understand about you?"

      He was trying to show me how to beat gravity
        when he said *Give me your arm.*

Let's say we do—we call opioids crossing the blood-brain barrier
wings. We grow wings
when we blow that barrier   open wide open—

the place where the bloodstream touches the eternal.
Is it going to hurt?

I remember how he said *The worst thing that could happen to you*
is nothing at all.

"Are you currently experiencing overwhelming sadness, grief or depression?"

I knew him five months before I knew
that past the night's black pulses
a river of light.
Never dreamed he would be the one to walk into it.

If lightning was going to strike
someone it should've been me.

In those five months, he overdosed twice—

what does it feel like to live

through the thing that's only going to kill you later?

"You cannot answer a question with a question."

The last night I saw him alive
        I had no idea I would never see him again.

People always want to say that they knew
        or that they had a feeling there was nothing
they could do
        to stop what was coming. I didn't.

People tell me his death *must've been a wake-up call.*
But why would it have been?

"You cannot answer a question with a question—"

The last night I saw him alive
I sat on the center island in the kitchen where, eight hours later,
        his heart would slur to a stop,
he would pitch
        into shock, coma—

I can see it without seeing it.
Apocalypse doesn't mean end
                it means *future*
brighter than where we are now. If I've learned anything
it's that lightning doesn't care
what the future has fated for us.

"Are you currently experiencing overwhelming sadness, grief or depression?"

You think you can help me, you think I'm here
so that you can ask but
I don't owe this story to anyone
not even you,
not even if it means helping myself.

Do you really need me to explain it?

Everyone has their own overdose story to draw from,
their own vision of being unable to save someone they love

from themselves.

"What then, do you hope to accomplish here?"

Why is his the voice I keep hearing? I can't sleep
the dead out of my head.
I can't sleep at all. His ghost feeds here
on the possibility of what

happened when he closed the door between us, when he finally was alone.
Was it ever possible for us to switch places?
Was it ever possible for us both to survive? Who chooses
who lives and who goes and how do I tell them that they chose wrong?

I still feel like I'm waiting for lightning.
The idea being if one shock was enough
to knock my mind spinning
off of its axis, another should be enough
to put it back, right?

BIRDS OF

"I loved you. I love you. You were.
 And you are."
—Mary Jo Bang, *Elegy*

No photos of us

looking happy—like we forgot
we were there. And still, I think about him when I'm not
even thinking.

I touch my face, the side of my throat   the places his hands have been
hold what I should forget   I remember

no canary in the coal mine, no proof but the water
acting weird again, smelling like blood, running at strange hours—
        no one else there

            when he stayed awake all night to check my pulse,
no one else illuminated   the cities at the center of me.

Did I dream up

birds of warning, birds of no   tomorrow, birds in my gut,
        in my hair, his hands in—   of his
kiss on every finger, his fingers to my pulse? It comes back

like the dead never will,

a between worlds pain   drags me.
I was 20 years old. I was vodka-drunk, out of my mind.

I was so calm.

He is the wound   without exit
—no voicemail to call,
             no clothes on my bedroom floor. All I have left

is a name I won't speak
because I don't want to wake

      the dead, don't want the dead

      to think I am moving on forgetting happy

MY LOVE IS A DEAD ARCTIC EXPLORER

Even when you rip the telephone from the wall

I still answer

the thought of your hands on me.
I say calmly to no one
$\qquad\qquad$ *this is going to hurt later.*

And that's not only because you have a temper,
because *yes, you do—*

or because
I'm all about the risk
that comes with this high—more fentanyl than anything—
white blare of bedsheets, our now of no nighttime,
a sky pasteurized by thunder

it's that desire never tells the truth,

it's that you and I both know *I want you*

is never enough.

We're up late, have been drinking.
$\qquad$ Once more

$\qquad\qquad$ the body is a glass

and from ourselves,
from the other
                    we drink

some impossible water.
        Tonight,

insomnia is the closest we'll come to a relationship with God.
Tonight, insomnia hits below the knees.

Insomnia is sexy

how morning never comes and there is no escape
from what we are:
                restless, x-ray blue light, phone waiting to ring,
                small minus sign of painkiller on the mirror between us.

Too late to take a Klonopin
the minute hand on the wall-clock falls,
                                struggles for the twelve.
Insomnia means I say half to the clock, half to you
don't start something you can't finish.

Insomnia means
                        you set aside my mind for my body.

I am calling myself
back from one type of brain damage
to you,

green awake against the dark,

our pulses ache.

Insomnia means never truly wake,
means that even if I do remember this later
all that will come back
are flashes—

my head against your chest,
                    can't get my dress off fast enough,

your fall of hair wound in my fists,
how you needed to hear the soft watts of your own name in the way I say it.

I am trying again
to learn what pleasure is—

                    it calls back to me

in every slurred
furious attempt
to have sex in present tense—

never real enough,
always three glasses of wine deep.

The grief in my head means it is easy to forget what I came for,
how I got here, what sign I misread
          means there are tracks on the threadbare
maps of my hips and I could try and tell you
exactly where they lead but you say:

Trees.

They remind you of trees. My body tells you

what I cannot: *A ring for each year—*

I stay tired
long after sleep.

My head is radioactive, you lay your hand flat against it.
You say: I *understand perfectly.*

I walk into your weather

knowing it means being the tree split by lightning because

     maybe sometimes love is supposed to hurt.

Maybe every time you enter
the tree is different.

One side you could wake me
with hands not over my mouth
but in—

     one side I am vomiting because I took too many painkillers,

one time
I did that to myself. Youth
is how we suffer without excuse,

an illness that blisters clouds
in front of a bloated moon.
Youth is inherently traumatic.

We can't do anything about that.

When you say you understand

you are trying to justify me to yourself
the nature of damage that two people can choose—
how that damage looks like a shotgun

      fired inside, how I bloody my fist against a wall because
      it feels so good.

OTHERLIGHT

Say

    only a light that blinks for years until it
hits land and casually stirs my sleep—

PSYCHOPHARMACOLOGY: LEVELS

"Tell me what you remember."

           In the beginning,

                there was sound—

"Are you talking about music?"

           No.
           A voice.

           A voice
                from that child's story said
                    Who is that trip-trapping on my bridge?

           He and I—we were sitting next to the swimming pool
           and all I could think was *I am so happy. I am so happy.*

                  I am going to have to pay for this happiness.
           How am I going to pay?

           Maybe that's when I knew
                something human to the bone—

           not the bone but the bone twisted beyond
           being twisted back.

I don't know the way back

to my body before this body
          before my body was changed
by antidepressants but if there is a way—

do I really want to find it?

There are levels
               to grief and happiness is one of them.

"Is it possible then that you are afraid to be happy?"

          From here I can pretend
                    that things last, that our lives will last

as long as mountains.

Childhood makes us so good at pretending I almost believe
that the dead might come walking back,
          might draw us a map to the place where their pulses went.

               Worlds don't last.

They lead us deeper with the belief

that this road, this bridge, this ladder, air, epoch
          will lead us safer.

I can pretend to believe or I can tell you the truth—

"And what is the truth?"

How else would death call me?

"Is that the question you are most afraid to be asked?"

Ask me if I miss him.

"Do you miss him?"

Healing means forgetting, means

what happened never happened.

Do I want that? No—*do I really want that?*

Water and time never belonged to me.

I hear myself
tell him my name.

When you fall in love with someone,
        you start speaking

the way they speak. I hear myself

say: *love means I can't stay here, love means*
            last night was a movie.

I've been told that when you fall
   in love it feels like flight—

as if love lasts long enough to grow wings.
     More often than not,

that fall kills you.

"When did you first come to this way of thinking?"

        August.

When what's left of sound

teases the graveyard. The worst part of loss is that you live
after it and my life

        has been annihilated by this loss.

I miss him and I have been
missing him and
I am allowed to be afraid that I will never be the same.

        What I need is a promise—

"What do you mean by promise?"

I want one less worry, I want someone to tell me

it will be okay, that a life after this one exists
and that he will find it—that I will find it—
even if we don't deserve it.
Is it so wrong

to want to be haunted?

"Pretend he is here, in this room right now. What would you say to him?"

I wake up still
> thinking you are alive—

my body gets used to that fog

as if you, as if the dead are nothing more
> than bones to the body. That pain is deep—

I will go deeper.

I stayed awake for months after you—

waiting
for your call
come back—people like you don't just disappear.
I would've waited forever

in the solstice cold, up
in the air, mountainside of disbelief if only to hear you say
my name.

Before you, I could not understand pain
> but I know it now and it sounds supernatural,
like beams of light
smashed across the small of my back. Sleep and never
sleep again
> where did you find yourself when you finally woke?

Did it hurt—?
      I mean is death anything like living?
Does it remind you of home?

I hope where you are is vast, real,

                    impossible—

a better oblivion,

          more sky—

I hope where you are is nothing
like home.

NOCTURNE

I tell a new doctor *wake me up.*

Let me feel close to the dead,
let me hear them
            tell me I was worth it

let them hear me say
I stop taking my antidepressants because I
long for awake.
I am exhausted

by a sane world clicking past
in increments of twelve hours,
twelve hours,
twelve—
repeat,
repeat.

        Repetition is a symptom of madness.

I stop because I want to feel something
that reminds me of how I felt before I lived
drugged,

meds standing between my body and the rest
of the world.

If it means hurting—*so what?*

If I can't feel—
what am I doing?
In the wild, animals use pain to survive

It would be a relief to be promised pain, some
strange comfort when the new doctor says:
"You've been high

for so long, coming down from that *well—*"

I'm not saying tonight ends with self
diagnosis, with healing.
I'm saying tonight's the night I take my life
                    into my own hands.

Lights blink once and out—I am at home thinking about the possibility of fire; the electrical wires' cooling glow in the dead museum of summer's ice.

Blistering took my palm—

I grow back a strange life in the dim of mines, shrapnel village of Mammoth bones, talk of eating the mules. I lick salt from the walls to stay alive. What if after life there can only be life?

I am way back in the way before the earth exposed her throat to me. When miners brought their small children down into the mines, to lay dynamite in places they could not reach. *Move quickly.*

Time is the only weapon you have. You don't want to be seen by it.

There were children boarded up behind the Icefall and left until Spring. When the miners returned the scratching had stopped.

Thought I would feel more or less at home in the underworld's mine, chewing corridors of salt, lithium— never mind the scythe

in every deep, another canary tastes for nerve gas, a chance for acid rain.

I throw myself down a staircase. Headfirst into blacking out, down here, attentive, in this school of the dead.

I ache for the sleep of a working salt mine. Mules were lowered by rope through ice-eaten night toward a single naked bulb, knowing

never again

would they rise,
only mineral
blistered tongue and down and down. I hear them in the mineshaft begin to recite the *Odyssey*—

If I am going to be unreasonable let me be all the way
                    unreasonable.

Do you ever feel like you will never die?

DREAM TREE

We are playing that child's game of *guess what I'm saying underwater,*

a game of who can stay
submerged longest,
      who can listen longest to the voices of the dead.

You say: *Give me your watch. I'll time you. How long can you hold—?*

And how precious is time,
how long wine waits to peak,
how long do we have
      before time fills our love with blood?

I look up at you across the swimming pool and I should not be afraid,
      I can see the bottom of the water
and it is safe and blue and clear
but already you are beginning to blur.

Time takes everything.
Wait with me, wait
for fingers of ice to climb you
the last possible moment
      before rising
            for air or to leave.

But how could I ever
leave you?

Who better
		knows my gravity? Who will love me knowing
the cost of love is love? Who else
loves me blackout
		drunk, out of my mind, vicious

with this rare, *never want this night to end,*
with this *leave your life,*
kind of love?

You bring me wine for my hangovers,
you call me back from
blood on the brain
		when I inhale too much water.

Time long stops the heart
This place
		is the place where you leave me.
I can't tell what you are shouting into the water
		but the question never was *what are you trying to say*

it is *how long will you stay*
knowing all that we are promised is loss.
Promise me

when you think of me
		you will think of me

as the river of light
		you would do anything to cross.
Promise me I will see you again
		even though I will never

see you again. We will never repeat—

       not in the same way,
not exactly,
not when more
       than a swimming pool stands between us.

Each time the dream comes after

I will have less.
I will go back
       to before I saw the sky.

I will take you with me
I will take you back

into this water. I will never move from this where,
this water where
       always

I find you.

—terrible to survive
and surviving is never over.

I keep hearing the sound
of a tree struck by lightning. The assignment

was to fall in love, love came to me
    differently, directly,

did me no good, changed me
for the worse.

    The world aches to say *Weren't you rescued?*

ON A CLEAR DAY

How quiet is Hell—how it unnerves you.

    Usually, panic throttles you
awake, anesthetizes,
      but today you wake up feeling.

        You do not expect gentleness—you expect birds

beating themselves blind against windows,
    no mouths. Driven mad-sex or sex

or Xanax or love, he tells you *there is worth*
in not feeling normal all the time.

Everything is yours for a while. Today
the neighbors are good neighbors.

Hell on a quiet day

is still Hell.
What is left to fear?

You are prepared for the end of restfulness:

birds waiting on the down power lines,
      birds on blown out chimneys, silent

opera of canaries—the birds always know first—

birds everywhere,

birds everywhere now.

PSYCHOPHARMACOLOGY: CLEAN

My prayer starts *Lord,*
I am powerless—

"Are you currently taking any psychiatric medication?"

Enough to kill

the thought of it
—overdose:

to over-give, to give utterly

to the unknown, to the pale

horse, pale flowers laid at the threshold
of a locked door

doesn't scare me anymore,

never made me want to change.
It made me bolder.

"Are you saying you find yourself participating in reckless behavior?"

I sound audacious

but I am afraid
that love made me weak.

I am afraid that this love made me weak.
I am afraid that it requires a sacrifice
            and the burned places on the scoop of my hips
were never enough.
The method

            by which a drug is introduced to your body determines
how quickly you'll leave
                        Paradise.

That's all I wanted—*want*—no matter how brief.
I'll take the half-life I've traded all senses for
that key that only opens one door—

            new wings at my back—dopamine—

what else could teach me

to read the sky,
keep me trying doors until dawn,
                hoping to follow him—*where?*—

and return? God is watching elsewhere.

            What can I get away with?

"Describe your current sleeping habits."

I overdo it—always

    with my hands in my own hair for comfort.

I talk to myself. I say *Lord, I am responsible.*
        Now I cover my own mouth with my hands.

Who wouldn't break? Is there more to life
than diacetylmorphine, strychnine cut with salt
        or sugar or rock white glowing seed of

ice—if I wake from it will I wake
in a body different
        than the body I leave behind?

He told me the overdose he lived through
        felt like a mountain.

"What do you think he meant by that?"

He meant no end.

    You get it if you've been to that peak
        where all sound
tightens around a barb of light, refuses
to let go.

"And how does that make you feel?"

High feels like high.

You want me to explain it?

I felt birds

      and atmosphere
too thin for wings,

      I thought *what pain*
as I fell

HISTORY OF SLEEP

When I sleep with a new you, I do not sleep. His breathing keeps me
        awake all hours. Dear

sleeping, I do not care.
You lonelied me. I wish he was you.

       The best I can do is guard his pulse. What I want most

in this life is my mouth against it, the inside of his wrist,
a heartbeat inside of my head—
                    my way of listening for history's repeat
because later, when I tell him my history,
     I will say *ghosts*.   I loved

your vaporized blood, blown out candles,
—feeling your way with frostbitten hands.

across a bottomless lake,

in the harrow of sleep. Every new man tastes like your name.

I would do anything
             to keep him—anything—
is not enough to keep him   alive. I listen
      to the horse beats of his heart rush him further.
Loss
      like your's—again, *can I take it?*
My rough, specific heart,

your image breaks   across my   hands. In the dark,
I will sing you,

you forever.
        Part of me knows this lullaby
                        is for me—still, I hope it carries
on the breath of the lake at dawn, on good ice,
to you,

    where the sleeping go—if you need

to go there, okay.   I need you to come back.

I WOULD SAY

When we started I thought
                    so that's the way light tastes.
I called light *future.*

        Now I feel its loss in my teeth, jaw, hands.
My hair still smells like your hair.
I can't think of my own body
            without thinking of yours,

without thinking of swimming pools lit
            by waves of lightning so close I can taste
their ozone and how there was a time when that taste was hope.

How many dawns did I greet hoping
            you had not stopped breathing in your sleep

or whatever we should call the blear
            between high and not high?

My love for you kept me awake.
    What little I knew then—
            watching over you, thinking that
                if you died I would want to die too.

I tried to love you like this: all or nothing.
How many times did I shake you back to me? Do you remember

what I said? I said
here is my only life—take it.

I mean if you're breathing, stay with me.
I mean if you're not
stay with me.

If your hand is in my hair, *leave it.*
If you are this hurt,
let it hurt. I can take it. Don't ever
be done with me.

OTHERLIGHT

What's wrong with me is wrong all the way—
white horses hesitant under my hand, they ask me if I mean it

when I tell them *they used to freeze people down here.*

I want the dread in stay, the light of a solar eclipse, and

you down here with me but please
        don't come here anymore, not like this.

I WOULD SAY

Do you think it impresses me
                    that you know how to hurt yourself?
You don't get to give up this life

for the otherworldwise.
I had faith that faith would be enough

to protect you from you. Faith is not a negotiation,
the sky is a lamp of blood. You gave your body to

a wilderness and the wild
   gave you oblivion. The night you died,

I called so many times I lost count.
         You didn't answer my panic then so
tell me now—
how long did the telephone ring
                    while you stared up at the ceiling fan,
boy who died choking,
blown out in a forest of pale mist?

                    It rang all night, didn't it?
When the landlord kicked your door open it was still ringing.
         When did you know

you were gone? When were you certain you couldn't take it back?
   What happened when you drank

from that milk river of forgetting?
Does forget mean forget
forever or did you learn everything

in the space of a single night,
in the seconds between ring and no answer?

IF I DON'T MEET YOU IN THIS LIFE, LET ME FEEL THE LACK

Almost no sound when I imagine
how your body might look through ice,

dazzling ice refracted back to snow.

Let me sleep then
            and dream of fish
or leopards or how every tree is a personality.
It is never about the sex

when you show up again—
                            backlit by the hallway light.
You don't ask to come in, you just are
and the most romantic thing I will ever do is to fuck you
while I am on a drug holiday.

I mean nothing between us. The world has always been ending,
I am getting what I asked for
when I asked for

your weather. I would give my body
for an instant of lightning. All night I try

to be a better person. Not for you—
maybe because of you—before you

I loved
        like a wild animal sees at night. I've been fortune told
that you will

abandon me slowly
like the cold pulling me through
the darkness or a confidence that leads me

but for one minute of fleeting life I put feathers to your birds.

The trail that led me was not of my making.
If it was the moon
        it fell
from my hands as you sleep with your back to me.

The earth is taking its time,
        is deciding how to kill us or how to change us—

I lay my hand flat
        against the perishable harp of your spine.

All night I ask you *why*. All night you tell me *no*.

I'LL LOVE YOU UNTIL THE END OF THE WORLD

The summit of Everest
    is the size of a dinner table.
We touch hands across it in the dim lit restaurant.

I always think of you as dead—

It hurts
to know and though there is always understanding
to be gained from pain,

I don't want this
    to be another night.
I don't want this to be how I last remember you.

Don't let this be the last time
    your hands gather on my face

like this—

not here,
not this passage of bread,

not my body filling, drowning
at 26,000—

while the scene is fading.
Say *Never leave me*
and I will live

forever
here with you even if it means being ice,

if it means taking off my clothes
in the no air here
and suffocating
on the monochromatic silence of sky

cooling, injured, beginning,
making ice

human,
my breathing clawing how I want it—

this glistering black mountain, graveyard of scaleless fish in the wind's tide, glowing
out from the spine.

In this you,
there can be no aftermath.

Why can't I stop
trying to prove love is more final than death?

The dead
don't like to be alone.
I like the climb—

the raw, the serac, the telephone ringing.
What is it—

the air, the lack
of it

or love
that has me eaten
by ice

        alive.

Say that is a once in a lifetime kind of pain—

a pain that only helps me understand other pain.
What happened to your mind?

What could happen to my own

this high up where the cameras stop working, where what is
captured on film is never believed?

You say to me *If you are sleepless, you are awake*
                in someone else's dream.
But what does it mean
     that I am dreaming of you?

I am dreaming of the dead.

On this planet of distance,
in this house of regret

the upper rooms are haunted and ghosts
     keep the lights on at strange hours,

never leave when asked.
never come when called.

The telephone is ringing and the dead on Everest answer:

I am so cold—please

don't cry. Everything will be fine.

       Why aren't you coming back?

Let me tell you what a ghost is—

I will

       stay awake
       against the things that want to hurt you.

I will talk out loud to keep them away—
to keep
the future begging
hands outstretched

for something to eat.

I TELL MY DEAD EX-BOYFRIEND'S MOTHER
THAT I WISH IT HAD BEEN ME

Believe me, it is easier to die
  than to watch someone you love die.

Believe me
  I have also braided my hair against pregnancy,
dared whatever god is watching to
do with me what you will.

And now, I am six months older
than he will ever be. I understand my body exists on luck
  alone. Like every night I started what I knew I couldn't finish,
bought what I couldn't pay for, what

I was never held responsible for.
I have never been a good person
but I am alive

and still learning how to live stunned cold by reality,
  slapped back again to breathing,

again and again to this world of prayers,
  world of charms and amulets, inevitable
like a cat brought back inside by the rain.
Whatever lives I have left
  I would offer your son.

When you heard did you fall against the shower?
    Did you wear your bedsheets like clothes?
Who did you bargain
with when you said *my life for his?* Who did you blame?
    Did you claw out your heart?   Did you? Did you, do you—

and *woman to woman*—tell me that you blame me. Still,
all this time, after him,
    I can't strip from my mouth the battery acid taste of guilt or
dead or dead or dead or—

love is so short. So forgetting. So long—
a gutter gathering rainwater, a lake,
    could be blood, could you forgive the rain?
    It rained all night.

PSYCHOTHERAPY: EPILOGUE

"What brings you back here?"

        I never thought I had escaped—
        thought *maybe*

        this was just the view from the precipice. I thought
        love could come without consequence. But of course,
        nothing is ever right

        in the lives of those who love each other.

"How long has it been since you last saw a therapist?"

        Perfection is a mental illness also.

            Or so people say—I'm convinced
        it's just discipline, correctness. I thought it would protect me
        in the way it did not protect you.

        I remember my mother making me practice
            my posture after grade school.

        She'd stack three books on top of my head.
        She'd point. She'd say "Walk."

And I would across the room
  back and back until I could move
without those books falling
Can still do it now.
  If this ever meant anything

it wasn't enough, though there was a time when
I believed it was
I miss that.

"What do you miss the most?"

I miss letting my body do what it wants.

"Can you be more specific?"

I mean in emergencies

I never know how to handle myself.

  When something is happening to you

what are you supposed to do, to say,

and how could I ever hope to stop the plan
God has coming for me
when just a few feet away
  a man throws his wife into a wall.

Maybe I shouldn't try and interpret violence.
Maybe, I play at tragedy

without believing the reality of it.

"Can you tell me how you spend your days? What are your interests? What is your work?"

Once, when he was still alive, I saw my future with him.

It was clean.
It was impossible, angels
        lit by polar auroras. I'll never get over it.
He kissed my hair to wake me, my face
against his shoulder.
I felt the heel of a child in the small of my back.

I'm allowed to be angry.

        Look at what's been lost.

"What have you lost?"

Maybe just knowing what could've been will be enough.
It will have to be. Though, a part of me wants to salvage
that life and another remembers

a couple arguing.

I heard them through the walls.
            Their children stood between them,

there was nothing I could do and *why*
do I say that when I don't really believe it?

I know what I heard.
I know what I heard.

"Did you know either of them? The couple in the dream?"

            Who said I was dreaming
            when I haven't slept in days?

            As for that couple
                    did I ever
            find out who they were

            and did I even want to?

            I think I know. I think I always knew.

"Are there people in your life you know you should spend less time with?"

            I want back that night, its delinquent thrill,
            its quiet—

so quiet—the very first night

was everything we wanted to do to each other.

There are so many rooms in that night,
everything lives in those rooms:

swimming pool, smoke, restaurants, snow,
jagged rocks—he used his entire body:
        teeth, jaws, bones, hands, nails.

It was ugly.

I did not know. Still—

I would've done anything.
I would still
       do anything.

"Is there a way you can expand on that? Tell me more."

    No.

"Overall, how would you describe your mood?"

Someone told me recently that human beings are divided
between those who want to move on, forward, and those
who keep looking back.

I would've died for him.
How many more ways must I say it?

Before him, I never wanted a life of waking up

but when someone you love touches you for the first time
you know you will kill
whatever stands between you and Paradise.
I feel guilty
that I am alive

when he is not. I am guilty

all of the awful things that I have done to stay alive.

I wish they were not true.

"If you could say anything to your future children, what would you?"

I would say *you*—

when I did these things I was thinking of you.

BETTER SKY

It would be best to forget
             all I have seen:
twin headed birds, ghosts of mules
shimmering with insomnia asking

Are we there yet?

Without him, only uncertainty is left for me.

I am almost done with this city now—
a memory is all that it will ever be.
That's fine.

When I get out of here it might be time to start
thinking about a new sort of life.

Perhaps I have learned enough to begin one
although I am not sure what
it is I have learned.

What have I learned? What have I learned
in this school of the dead?
And where to begin?

Let me begin

not at the beginning, not even at the wake. But
rather at the I *will never again*

posses the conviction of children that
nothing terrible will ever happen to me.
    I will never again feel

that endless aquifer of birds under my skin
delighted and oblivious—

From now on it can only be:

"What have I done?"

"What myths will the land write for itself?—"

like every living creature that ventures
so far from home.

If there is anything I can leave you with it's that
there is water down here,

running under us, rivers that children wade into
and do not return from as children.

I don't want to say goodbye to you

but I can't take another night, another flashback
to the rooftop swimming pool looking over Millennium Park,
trees wrapped in lights
        can't take another illusion

of permanence.
        I love you so much and I don't want to leave you
but I am still hoping to live, still hoping to be
something—someone I don't have to be sorry for.

        I'm sorry—
I promise I will talk to you every day,
I will answer
        the telephone when it rings. I will write letters,

carve your name in the ice, stand in the rain, look always for your ghost—
though you've waded so far past where my feet can touch.

I won't forget.

Once, there were fish

                        waiting in ice caves under the mountains
for a gradual magic that would turn them into birds.

        Their bodies glowed—white eggs of spiders,

signposts in the maze leading on
                    from the caves of the earth into a changing world.

When it's over—*and it is over*—
                            let me think of salt,
of tree, of lightning, of ice, golden sky.
Let me believe it better for there to exist
some things that once changed,

                            cannot be changed back.

TREETOPS

Wine glasses on your nightstand. You've been gone
six months now but I still sleep
in your bed. I feel closest to you
      when I swallow the pills and blunt the knife, keep me
from hearing your voice.

      I sleep in my dress again,
I sleep in the snow and listen
for that sound of the screen tearing
      on the window: *come to me from where*

you are. Say It's been a long day
      because it has been a long day, hasn't it? A long week, a long life—

and I will spend that walk home thinking about your hands.
Maybe, from this road,

      I will write letters.
I will write: *So tell me*
        how I am supposed to go only forward, only rise
to stars,
      to follow this path without you?

Maybe I will stay
      here. Maybe I will heal.

I will believe the divine—the lisdexamfetamine, buproprion, ziprasidone—
            will start working again. Maybe this is the last of the snow
and the path will clear.

I ask you *Do you think it will ever be enough?*
Do you think the world will stay wild?
                Do you think I will
find a way to live in it?

It's better if I leave it alone, better if I can't name it.
        It is better if I never find my way
back to this moment.

Tomorrow will cool me with grey light, will wake me
with ice. My hands will not shake,
                I will talk to my visions
my symptoms will steady me—

I won't worry about how I might become someone
                no one
                        could ever live through.

The title of "The Lake Will Wait" is made in reference to Gwendolyn Brooks's poem "To the Young Who Want to Die"

"Bound For" is after Ursula Le Guin

"Dynamite" refers to a mixture of cocaine and heroin

"Telephone" makes reference to Richard Wilbur's poem "Love Calls Us to the Things of this World"

The phrase "stylishly drowning" in the poem "Drowning Does Not Look Like Drowning" is made in reference to Simeon Barry's book "Ampersand Revisited."

The line "All night I ask you why. All night you tell me no" is directly quoted from Alejandra Pizarnek's poem "(All night I hear the water sobbing)"

"My Life is a Dead Arctic Explorer" is titled after Paige Ackerson Keily's book of the same title and is written after Simeon Berry

"Dream Tree" is after Keith S. Wilson

"If I Don't Meet You in This Life, Let Me Feel the Lack" is taken from the film *The Thin Red Line*

"I'll Love You Until the End of the World" is titled after the painting of the same name by Josh Keys

"Psychotherapy: Epilogue" makes reference to Louise Glück's poem "Faithful and Virtuous Night"

ACKNOWLEDGMENTS

Thank you to my family—blood and chosen—for your support and love during the living and writing of this book.

Thank you to Caroline Chavatel, Tyler Julian, Brooke Sahni, Joy David, Joshua Young, Nate Wilkerson, Richard Greenfield, Connie Voisine. You are brilliant readers, critics, poets, editors, and teachers—you are even better friends.

Thank you to everyone at YesYes Books. You are a dream.

Thank you to the publications in which these poems have previously appeared:

The Lake Will Wait *Zocalo Public Square*
Bound For *Muzzle Magazine*
Drowning Does Not Look Like Drowning (originally titled The Swimming Pool)
    Moonchild Magazine
Dynamite *Ghost City Review*
Telephone *Okay Donkey*
Psychopharmacology: Levels *Up the Staircase Quarterly*
I Would Say . . . I wake up still thinking you are alive . . . *Glass: A Journal of Poetry*
Dream Tree and Birds Of *The Shore*
Noon, Midnight, Doves (*White Stag Publishing Firebrand Anthology*, 2021)
My Love is a Dead Arctic Explorer (Anti-Heroin Chic Magazine, as well as inclusion
    in Anti Heroin Chic's Anthology)
I Would Say . . . when we first started . . . (Burning House Magazine)
I'll Love You Until the End of the World *Longleaf Review*
Better Sky & I Would Say . . . think I want to say goodbye . . . *Rabid Oak*
Treetops *Bodega Magazine* 2020

JILL MCELDOWNEY is the author of the full-length collection *Otherlight* (YesYes Books, 2023) and the chapbook *Airs Above Ground* (Finishing Line Press, 2018). She is a founder and editor of Madhouse Press. Her previously published work can be found in journals such as *Prairie Schooner*, *Fugue*, *Vinyl*, *Muzzle*, and other notable publications.

Another Way to Split Water by Alycia Pirmohamed

One God at a Time by Meghan Privitello

I'm So Fine: A List of Famous Men & What I Had On by Khadijah Queen

If the Future Is a Fetish by Sarah Sgro

Gilt by Raena Shirali

Say It Hurts by Lisa Summe

Boat Burned by Kelly Grace Thomas

Helen Or My Hunger by Gale Marie Thompson

As She Appears by Shelley Wong

RECENT CHAPBOOK COLLECTIONS

Vinyl 45s

    Inside My Electric City by Caylin Capra-Thomas

    Exit Pastoral by Aidan Forster

    Of Darkness and Tumbling by Mónica Gomery

    The Porch (As Sanctuary) by Jae Nichelle

    Juned by Jenn Marie Nunes

    Unmonstrous by John Allen Taylor

    Preparing the Body by Norma Liliana Valdez

    Giantess by Emily Vizzo